Max and Sam

by Rebecca Blankenhorn
illustrated by Barry Mullins

Core Decodable 34

McGraw Hill Education

Bothell, WA • Chicago, IL • Columbus, OH • New York, NY

MHEonline.com

Send all inquiries to:
McGraw-Hill Education
8787 Orion Place
Columbus, OH 43240

ISBN: 978-0-02-135391-0
MHID: 0-02-135391-3

Printed in Canada.

9 10 11 12 KOD 24

Max and Sam fix stuff.

Max and Sam fix a box.

Max can rub a sax.

Can Sam rub a sax?

Max and Sam fix a fox.

Last, Max can list stuff.

1. Fix a box
2. Rub a sax
3. Fix a fox